Come and talk with me

A collection of conversations between Mina Drever and some
residents at Redbond Lodge Residential Care Home

Mina Drever

Published in England by MinaDrever Limited

ISBN: 978-1-3999-1133-7 (paperback)
ISBN: 978-1-3999-1132-0 (ebook)

Cover image by Mykola Nisolovskyi/dreamstime.com

MINA DREVER
All enquiries to be sent to: minadrever@aol.com
Published by MinaDrever Limited
England
November 2021

This book is dedicated to the families of the people who shared their mental lives with me in these pages

Thank you

CONTENTS

FOREWORD
By Sue King

I would like to thank Mina on behalf of all the residents and staff for all her hard work and support which has highlighted the way we look at Dementia and the importance of listening and understanding the reasons behind behaviours.

I feel this book could be an excellent training tool.

I really hope that, in time, the word Dementia will be removed and Amelesia will be used.

Sue King was the manager at Redbond Lodge Residential Care Home in Great Dunmow until August 2021. She had worked at Redbond Lodge for twenty-four years. All my Amelesia work was carried out at Redbond Lodge with her enthusiastic and unstinting support. She said that she was brought to tears reading these conversations.

WELCOME

I hope you enjoy reading these conversations as much as I have enjoyed writing them down.

I had been visiting residents living in Redbond Lodge Residential Care Home in Great Dunmow for over five years when COVID-19 invaded our homes and our lives, and I had to stop my twice-weekly visits.

Many of the ladies and gentlemen with whom I sat and chatted had become my friends as much as I had become, to a few of them, the only visitor that brought a welcome distraction from their mental loneliness.

With the coronavirus lockdown, unable to continue with these visits, I decided to recall some of these conversations and write them down from memory so that I could give a voice to those who feel that their thoughts and feelings are often dismissed as meaningless meanderings – and also to pay homage to them.

I wish to emphasise that these conversations were never recorded. They were not interviews. No scripts exist of these chats. When I say that I have written them down from memory, I mean exactly that. I have sat and chatted with many people over the course of five years and more. I do not recall all of them. The five conversations in the first section of this book and the two in the fourth section were repeated so many times that I have only to visualise the person in my mind and they all come flooding back, with the hesitations, the voice tremors, the shrugs of the shoulders, the welling-up in the eyes, the smiles, the delights of just talking and being listened to. I can see them and hear them all so clearly.

The third section of the book – the incidental conversations – contains a few brief encounters, unplanned yet forceful in their vehemence. I can see the faces and hear the voices, but not the names. They were just that, incidental yet powerful in the messages I was receiving.

The families of the people with whom I had the seven conversations in sections one and four have kindly given permission for me to publish them in this book. They have read the conversations and they have not changed a word. From this I take comfort that I have been faithful to their relative's words. I am grateful. I hope you will come to appreciate the force in the words of these few people. I believe they represent the mental lives of millions of people worldwide whose minds are incapacitated by brain diseases.

WHY WRITE DOWN THESE CONVERSATIONS?

When I chatted with the people in these little scenarios, I wanted to get to know each person because I am curious about people's lives, what makes them who they are, how they got here, to this point in their lives.

For as long as I can remember, I have been fascinated by the power of life's experiences that older people could talk about. As a young girl, I would sit enthralled by older relatives and friends of my parents as they recounted stories of life's experiences that sounded adventurous to my unworldly imagination. My interest in the world took root not in books or in television or in magazines, but in the lives of the older people in my young life. I am now an older person in many young people's lives. I am still fascinated by other people's life adventures – whether as shopkeepers, cleaners, civil servants, doctors, hairdressers, mothers, fathers – because each person's life is fascinating.

Many people – including those in the medical profession – have difficulty talking with relatives or friends or patients whose mental and verbal abilities have been disabled by neural disturbances in their brains. As I got to know residents in Redbond Lodge Care Home, the managers would often ask me to visit particular people because they seemed unhappy or distressed. I would report back my conversations, and the managers would often act on issues that might have had a bearing on a person's well-being. For example, a resident might be worried about a family member and wish someone to call the family on their behalf; or a carer might have been inadvertently (occasionally not inadvertently) verbally unkind; or they might just want someone to sit and chat. Residents are acutely aware that carers are so busy with so many people to care for.

Sue King, the general home manager at Redbond Lodge, would often say that residents would tell me things they didn't tell carers. I began to wonder whether I used language in a fundamentally different way that engaged people. I became aware of this whilst I was writing a memoir[1] of my mother's life during her 'dementia years', as I used to call them.

I began to work on an idea that I had had for quite some time and which I discussed with the manager at Redbond Lodge, Sue King. With Sue's support, I developed my idea into a short training programme for sixth form students on how to

---

1 The memoir is called *Thank you lady* by Mina Drever, published by Austin Macauley and available on Amazon.

hold good conversations with people living with Alzheimer's or similar conditions.

THE STUDENTS AND THE TRAINING PROGRAMME

The students came from Felsted School, near Great Dunmow. We had workshops on how to use our language in a slightly different way, and how to listen, in order to have a two-way conversation with people living with memory loss and mental confusion. They were amazed at how easy it was to involve some of the residents, whom they visited, into meaningful conversations that made sense.

The students were also astonished to discover that – contrary to what they were growing up to learn from the media and from general talk around them in society – these residents they met were not 'mad' as the word 'dementia' suggests that they might be.

After this experience, the students agreed with me that the word 'dementia' is not a good word and they liked my suggestion that maybe we could use a different word, one that I constructed: *Amelesia.* The manager at Redbond Lodge liked it very much too and believes that the whole world should adopt it.

Amelesia means unmindfulness. I suggest that people affected by Alzheimer's or by Lewy Body or by Huntingdon's Disease are not able to concentrate on conversations in the normal way, because the damage to their brains makes it difficult for them to focus their mind on anything for any length of time. In other words, they are not capable of being 'mindful'. So, they find themselves in a state of unmindfulness.

We, the students and I, agreed that it is possible to hold and sustain good conversations with 'brain-damaged people' (because that's what Alzheimer's and similar conditions do – they damage our brains) if we adjust the words we use and the way we say them, listening carefully, picking up cues and giving time for people to decide on an answer.

An unexpected result of this type of conversation is that, through the exchange of simple language and through simple listening and picking up cues, we find incredibly strong characters that have been somewhat diminished by society's attitudes towards people diagnosed with 'dementia'.

I will wager that readers of these conversations will have encountered professionals who have told them that the 'mother', the 'husband', the 'grandmother' is not the person that one used to know: he/she has gone. I have been challenging this attitude for a very long time since my mother was diagnosed with 'vascular dementia'. I realised very early on in this new life of hers that 'vascular dementia' was a licence to ignore the stories she would tell as imaginings of her 'demented' mind.

The students who visited and chatted with some of the residents living with mild to medium degree of mental decline because of a brain disease were astonished to find indomitable characters delighted to talk about themselves. They just need a nudge for them to open up, in jolts and starts, maybe, and share their precious experiences.

A FUSION OF TIME AND SPACE

I noticed one particular and striking aspect of the mind affected by Alzheimer's and similar diseases: each person's life is affected by some powerful event or events that remain indelibly etched in the person's memory structures of the brain. Those memories seem to appear to the fore of people's mind unbidden and at surprising moments. They seemingly have no bearing to what might be going on all around. These events are so vividly expressed, it's as if I am experiencing them with the person telling me their stories.

For example, see my conversation with Millie in Section One, who suddenly wanted to share her big 'secret' with me one morning in the midst of me asking her what she would like for breakfast. She had her eyes shut when I spoke to her. Had she been reliving this secret in her mind? Or did something in my tone or my voice remind her of someone else's voice? Someone who had been with her at the moment of this secret? Something must have triggered this memory and she was experiencing it as if it were for the first time. Millie had two children. She had grandchildren. She was reliving that moment as if it were happening at that very moment. She was no longer, just for a moment, a lady with severe physical and mental disabilities: she was a radiant young new mum. Who was I to deny her that momentary joy? I was witnessing what I call a *fusion of time and space,* which occurs in our mind as a result of brain damage in our brain's physical structure. We are not simply recalling; we are reliving that moment as if it were now.

The idea that our mind wanders through the experiences of our life in a different way when healthy and when damaged by brain diseases came to me when my mother's brain was damaged by vascular dementia. I observed an amazing phenomenon taking place right in front of me: my mother merged memories from long ago with a present moment as if they were one and the same experience. For example, see her conversation with my sister Lucia about Lucia's sons in Section Three. My mother knew that her daughter had two sons, but in her mind, they were small children. Though her daughter in front of her at the moment of the conversation was obviously a much older woman than the young mother she had been, our mother's mind merged a fact from her past with the present experience and remembered that someone was looking after her young grandsons.

I started to imagine my mother's 'mental meanderings' as a fusion of time and space. I was not aware then of the theories of time and space in astrophysics. I never studied physics and my knowledge is limited to what I learn from TV programmes such as those presented by Brian Cox[2] in *Wonders of the Universe.*

A few years ago, while idly listening to the radio, I heard an Italian theoretical physicist, Carlo Rovelli, talk about time and space in the universe being one dimension in which there is no past, no present, no future. He talked about a 'continuous present'.

I wondered if my mother saw her life, in her mind, as a continuous present, with no clear demarcation of what had happened at different times and different places. In one sentence she would often talk about people and events of previous times as if they were taking place 'now', in the presence of people that were present in 'both times' – the past and the now.

This is difficult to explain. I talk in my memoir that my mother seemed (to me) to see her whole life like a film in which the scenes have a cohesive meaning but no sequence. When the scenes took place becomes irrelevant. Only the WHOLE story matters. How and when they took place does not.

I started to read more about time and space in popular science books after this first encounter with Carlo Rovelli on the radio. I began to ask myself whether my mother's mind, operating now in a physically damaged brain, was a reflection of

---

2 At the time of writing this, September 2021, Brian Cox is professor of particle physics at the University of Manchester, UK.

space-time in the universe where there is no past, no present, no future. Only this harmonious vastness of 'happenings', which is eternally 'there'.

Does our life show itself, in our damaged brain, as a 'wholeness' that is eternally present, (while we live) in our minds? Do we see distinct 'pieces' highlighted as we scan it, just as we might scan a panorama with binoculars: different bits come into focus as we move the binoculars?

Apparently, some physicists have been considering whether our brains see our lives' events as a film. The neuroscientist Dean Buonomano in his book *Your brain is a time machine*[3] considers this idea with reference to some of these physicists. He quotes (on page 171) one physicist called Julian Barbour describing watching a kingfisher in flight:

> My brain contains, at any one instant, several 'snapshots' at once. The brain … somehow 'plays the movie' for me … I see … six or seven snapshots of the kingfisher just as they occurred in the flight I saw. This brain configuration, with its simultaneous coding of several snapshots, nevertheless belongs to just one …

Julian Barbour is saying that when our brain sees something happening with an object or animal or person in it, the brain makes immediate links to other times when the same object/animal/person were observed, and multiple images present themselves to the mind at the same instant.

This was happening in my mother's brain. Her mind,

---

3 *Your brain is a time machine: the neuroscience and physics of time*, by Dean Buonomano, published by W W Norton and Company in 2018.

operating in her damaged brain, was not sequencing the events in the order they might have happened as known to other people who might have been familiar with those events. Her mind was making emotional and factual connections of events. The timing of these events was blurred. They overlapped with one another. But they made sense to her. And they made sense to me because I had known her life. I knew she was not inventing people.

We see this phenomenon in the conversations with the residents of Redbond Lodge in this book. The seemingly erroneous and irrational anecdotes may have a factual basis in the life of the person with whom we are chatting. They must not be dismissed as meaningless imaginings. We must respect them. They are a life that has been lived. Memories come to mind a bit like pieces of a jigsaw puzzle. If we listen carefully, over time, we can create a complete picture of a person's life.

I AM STILL ME

I hope you will discover, as I did, that the person living with mental confusion and poor mental co-ordination of thought is still the person he or she used to be, in some form, in some way: it's up to us to find that person through conversation.

It does not matter how tiny the fragment of revelation that we may hear of this long and lived existence is. There might just be something that is revealed that you never knew about because we are, each one of us, more than just the person that others may think they know.

Here is a quote by Carlo Rovelli, the Italian astrophysicist that I mentioned above. He writes very clearly about what time and space in our universe are and how they relate to how we humans think of spacetime and how we develop and change with the flow of time. He says in one of his books that we should not be constrained by a simplistic idea of who and what we are, because:

> We are histories of ourselves. Narratives. I am not this momentary mass of flesh reclined on the sofa, typing the letter 'a' on my laptop; I am my thoughts full of the traces of the phrases that I am writing; I am my mother's caresses, and the serene kindness with which my father calmly guided me; I am my adolescent travels; I am what my reading has deposited in layers in my mind; I am my loves, my moments of despair, my friendships, what I have written, what I have heard; the faces engraved on my memory. I am, above all, the one who a minute ago made a cup of tea for himself. The one who a moment ago typed the word 'memory' into his computer. The one who just composed the sentence that I am now completing. If all this disappeared, would I still exist? I am this long, ongoing novel. My life consists of it.[4]

---

4   This quote is by an Italian astrophysicist who writes beautifully about what time is in our universe and how we humans understand time. I read him to try and understand how our brain's system of memory works with respect to how time is understood to function in the universe. I confess to being quite overwhelmed. But I love his thoughts on what we really are.

   The order of time by Carlo Rovelli, published by Penguin Random House UK in 2018. The quote is on page 154.

ORGANISATION OF THE CONVERSATIONS

I have organised these conversations into four sections:

1. Section One contains conversations with five residents at Redbond Lodge Residential Care Home displaying varying degrees of difficulties with recall and confusion, but who would otherwise be quite articulate.
2. Section Two contains conversations with my mother: these are extracts from the memoir *Thank you lady* that I wrote (see footnote 1). I carried out an extensive analysis of the language used in conversations between my mother and other people; this analysis informed the training programme that I wrote for the students from Felsted School.[5]
3. Section Three contains incidental conversations at Redbond Lodge with four residents; they are exactly what the title says – incidental – because they were not planned visits. They took place the once; they were very memorable.
4. Section Four contains two conversations with two other residents at Redbond Lodge before COVID-19 struck us. I visited these two ladies over a period of some years; they

---

5 If you are interested in reading about this training programme, you can find it on my website www.amelesia.com

enjoyed my visits and chit-chats as much as I enjoyed their company with laughter and, sometimes, barely concealed frustration on their part and helplessness on my part. Two indomitable characters in very discrete ways – their physical needs betrayed their fiercely alive brains.

NOTE: I have obtained permission to publish from the families of the five conversations in Section One and the two conversations in Section Four. The four incidental conversations in Section Three are anonymised. I never knew the names of these individuals. I gave them fictitious names.

SECTION ONE:
CONVERSATIONS WITH

five residents at Redbond Lodge with varying degrees of mental impairment: Cherryl, Patsy, Terry,
Pam, Millie

Conversation with Cherryl

Cherryl is tall and unsteady on her feet because of her poor eyesight. She walks with the help of a walking frame. She takes care to maintain a straight, firm posture. She has straight, broad shoulders and a strong face. As I get to know her over the years, I can see in my mind the very efficient business manager and the resolute woman she must have been. I learn that she had managed the family builder's yard, which she and her husband set up to become a successful concern in the town where they had lived as a young married couple. With business success came a comfortable lifestyle dotted with cruises and golf. Cherryl had loved her cruises, but she rarely talks about them, unless specifically asked to do so.

Cherryl talks constantly about her husband. They had been married fifty-two years by the time I had to suspend my visits to the care home because of the advent of COVID-19 in March 2020. From my conversations with Cherryl over the years, I felt that she and her husband had had a good, solid partnership imbued with respect for each other's strengths and acceptance of each other's foibles. There is always a tinge of sadness when she talks about him because she had been forcibly taken away from him to come to live in this residential care home. Cherryl is very sad about her current situation and tries very hard to accept it with equanimity.

This conversation takes place every time I see Cherryl, with hardly any word change. There might be some addition or omission at different times, depending on the amount of time that I spend with Cherryl. We often have a shortened version as I serve her breakfast, or as we walk to or from her room on the second floor of the residential home. The content and words hardly ever alter, because this is what is constantly at the forefront of Cherryl's mind. Her life is spent thinking about this.

Mina: Good morning Cherryl, how are you today?
Cherryl: Oh, hello dear, how lovely to see you. (Cherryl holds out her hand to grasp mine)
Mina: It's good to see you too, Cherryl. How are you today?
Cherryl: Yes, I'm alright … well, you've got to be, haven't you? Stuck in here … tell me, do you know when I'm going home?
Mina: I have no idea, Cherryl. Why, are there any plans for you to go home?
Cherryl: Probably not … but I shouldn't be here, I should be at home, looking after my husband.
Mina: Where is your husband, Cherryl?
Cherryl: Well, he's at home … he's probably playing golf! (Cherryl laughs).
Mina: Where is that Cherryl, where is your home?
Cherryl: Oh dear, not far from here, in Sawbridgeworth.
Mina: Have you lived there long?
Cherryl: Oh, now you're asking me, quite a long time. We used to live in Edmonton.
Mina: Never heard of Edmonton Cherryl, where is that?
Cherryl: In North London, near Epping. We had a builder's

	yard. Yes. (Cherryl tugs at my hand). I don't know why I am here. I shouldn't be here.
Mina:	Why did you come here, Cherryl?
Cherryl:	It was an accident, I know it was, it couldn't have been anything else.
Mina:	What accident? Did you fall down?
Cherryl:	Noooooh, he threw away my tablets. He didn't mean to do it, I know. He's not evil.
Mina:	(I wait … Cherryl shakes her head … she holds my hand the whole time) Who Cherryl, who threw away your tablets?
Cherryl:	My husband, but he didn't mean to do it, he's a good man. He misheard me talking on the telephone with my friend … she took the same tablets as me … I was telling her that I didn't want to take them any more … and he threw them away … but he didn't mean to do it … I know, he's not nasty. (Cherryl rubs my hand) … Oh it's good to talk … tell me again dear? What is your name?
Mina:	Mina. I'm Mina, Cherryl.
Cherryl:	Oh yes Mina, such a lovely name! I shouldn't forget it … I shouldn't forget it (Cherryl taps my hand). You're all so lovely here … don't get me wrong … everybody is really good here, I couldn't fault them for anything, but really dear … I shouldn't be here. … I should be at home looking after him?
Mina:	Your husband?
Cherryl:	Hmmm … he's not very well.
Mina:	What's the matter with him?
Cherryl:	He's got cancer
Mina:	What sort?

Cherryl: Oh, it's prostrate.
Mina: Has he had it a long time?
Cherryl: No not really … I can't remember. I guess that's why I am in here? Because he can't look after me … but I should be at home with him.
Mina: Why can't you look after him, Cherryl?
Cherryl: Well … I can't do much … I have got this eye condition … I can't see very well …
Mina: What is it called, your eye condition?
Cherryl: Oh, I can't remember. I can't see you at all.
Mina: Not at all? Not even a shadow?
Cherryl: I can see your shadow, but I can't see anything on the sides … I can't see from the corner of my eyes. It's a genetic condition. My sister has got the same condition. But not as bad.
Mina: So, you've always had it?
Cherryl: Yes … but it's got worse … I take tablets for it … have I had my tablets?
Mina: I don't know, Cherryl; shall I find out?
Cherryl: Would you? I should take them first thing in the morning you know. I think that's why I'm here, you know. They've changed my tablets, when I take them.
Mina: I'll ask the nurse in the office.
Cherryl: Would you? And, when you do, will you ask her when I'm going home?
Mina: I don't think I can do that, Cherryl … they won't tell me … I am not your family or carer … Maybe your family can ask? Your husband? When is he coming next to visit you?
Cherryl: I don't know … I'm not sure if he comes … he's not well you know …. I should be at home looking after him.

Mina: What about your daughter, Cherryl? When is she coming to visit?

Cherryl: I don't know, she's so busy, she comes to do my hair … and that's another thing …

Mina: What?

Cherryl: He got annoyed because she got married again?

Mina: Who got married again, Cherryl?

Cherryl: My daughter … and I say, it's her business. He's not right to be annoyed.

Mina: Who's annoyed with your daughter, Cherryl, for getting married again?

Cherryl: Him, her father!

Mina: Your husband?

Cherryl: Yes …. (Cherryl laughs) … it's none of his business … she's a grown woman.

Mina: (We laugh together).

Cherryl: It's good to see you dear (Cherryl squeezes my hand). What's your name again dear?

Mina: It's Mina, Cherryl.

Cherryl: Such a pretty name … Nina.

Mina: Mina with an 'm' for mum.

Cherryl: Mina … Mina … I should remember that! Such an unusual name, Mina.

Mina: Well, I have to go now, Cherryl.

Cherryl: Alright dear, thank you for coming … so nice to talk to someone, don't get me wrong, everybody is very good, very nice here, but I shouldn't be here, honest to God, I should be at home with my husband. When do you think I might go home?

Mina: I don't know, Cherryl. I'll ask in the office. I'll ask someone to come and have a chat with you.

Cherryl:	Will you? Oh, thank you. You're so kind.
Mina:	Okay, I have to go now, my husband is waiting for me in the car park.
Cherryl:	Alright dear. What's your name again?
Mina:	It's Mina.
Cherryl:	Mina.
Mina:	Bye, Cherryl.
Cherryl:	Bye bye, dear

When I resume my visits in May 2021, I find Cherryl, to my delight, displaying the same concerns for her husband. I understand. My mother was exactly the same: a devoted wife and life partner, obsessed with wanting to care for her husband, unable to comprehend why she could not. We pick up the conversation where we left it before COVID-19 – with one difference: her memory is not as strong as it was before COVID. Cherryl is often in tears because she does not know if her husband is alive or dead. It breaks my heart to say, 'I don't know Cherryl'.

Conversation with Patsy

Patsy is tall, slim and good looking. She likes to keep her hair short, which is cut and styled to frame her chiselled face perfectly. Patsy is given to walking up and down corridors by herself, deep in thought. She likes to hold and cuddle soft toys and she loves to feel soft materials. When the care home manager acquires tactile resources for people living with Alzheimer's and similar conditions, she does so with Patsy in mind.

Patsy appears calm and contemplative. Most of the time, she is. Occasionally, she will lash out to carers, as if to protect herself from harm and to defend herself in the face of contradictions. I was told that she had suffered some emotional trauma later in life, which had affected her deep psyche. She responds particularly strongly to castigating tones used by some carers. For example, occasionally, a carer might say 'you can't do that Patsy, that's naughty', if Patsy pushes away with her hand a carer's gesture, such as offering a biscuit. You can feel her sense of injustice when she thinks that she is not being spoken to with a respectful tone.

I have occasional, very short chats with Patsy. Most of the time she is happy just sitting in companiable silence.

Here are a few chats I had with Patsy at different times.

Mina: (I pull up a chair next to Patsy) Hello, Patsy.
Patsy: Oh hello.

Mina:	Can I sit with you for a minute?
Patsy:	If you want (Patsy smiles).
Mina:	He's a beautiful cat! (Patsy is holding and stroking a white furry cuddly toy).
Patsy:	Yes, it's a she.
Mina:	Oh, okay, a she cat?
Patsy:	Hmm … (smiles).
Mina:	What's her name?
Patsy:	I can't remember …
Mina:	Oh … is she not your cat?
Patsy:	No … she just arrived … from somewhere …
Mina:	What's the matter Patsy? (Patsy has tears in her eyes; she is holding a small soft rug and angrily pulling imaginary stuff from it)
Patsy:	It's here?
Mina:	It's here?
Patsy:	It's her, isn't it?
Mina:	Her?
Patsy:	Yes, her.
Mina:	Did she upset you?
Patsy:	Yes.
Mina:	How did she upset you?
Patsy:	She shouldn't say that.
Mina:	You are right, Patsy; she shouldn't have said that.
Patsy:	No.
Mina:	What did she say exactly?
Patsy:	I can't remember.
Mina:	I don't know her, Patsy; who is she?
Patsy:	I don't know her either (Patsy looks at me and I can see a shadow of a smile).

Mina:	Is she in this room?
Patsy:	No, she's gone.
Mina:	That's good, isn't it?
Patsy:	Yes.
Mina:	Now she can't upset you anymore.
Patsy:	No, that's right.
Mina:	Would you like to go for a walk, Patsy?
Patsy:	Alright then.
Mina:	(I help Patsy out of her chair, and we go for a walk around the corridors downstairs on the ground floor and we stop and chat to people we encounter; Patsy recovers her good humour).
Mina:	Good morning, Patsy, you look happy today! (Patsy smiles at me as I stand with her by the window and look out).
Patsy:	Good morning … how are you?
Mina:	I am okay, Patsy, how about you? How are you today?
Patsy:	I am okay, yes … it's a lovely day.
Mina:	It is, Patsy … look at that sky … not a hint of a cloud.
Patsy:	No … (Patsy turns and walks back to a chair and sits down).
Mina:	I saw that you had visitors yesterday, Patsy, while I was here.
Patsy:	Yes … yes, I did.
Mina:	Who were the ladies sitting with you?
Patsy:	I can't remember … my sister, I guess.
Mina:	There was a younger woman who looked like you; was that your daughter?
Patsy:	How do you know my daughter?

Mina: I don't know her.

Patsy: Oh …

Mina: How do you get on with your daughter?

Patsy: Good … yes … what about you?

Mina: Me? I don't have a daughter, Patsy … I have a son.

Patsy: That's nice.

Mina: And I have two grandchildren, Patsy.

Patsy: That's nice.

Mina: Do you have any grandchildren, Patsy?

Patsy: Huu? … I'm not sure. (Patsy is beginning to rub her eyes, which she does when she is tired).

Mina: I'll leave you to have a rest now, Patsy. I'll see you next time I come. Okay?

Patsy: Okay.

The key to Patsy's good humour is a warm, kind tone without sounding condescending. She enjoys short chats and quiet company. She is much loved by some of the carers.

Conversation with Terry

Terry is a very gentle person. He is very precise in his movements and in the management of his surroundings and of his possessions. He has papers and folders that contain drawings and photographs of objects and people that have played major roles in his life. Chief among these are airplanes and men standing near airplanes. Terry has books on airplanes and magazines about airplanes. All these items have their own place, and Terry knows exactly where they are when he wants to show me any of them.

Terry is measured in the way he speaks. He nods when I ask him a question, spends some time thinking about it and then gives an appropriate answer, which is usually very short, simply a yes or no, or just a repetition of words I use. I do not know the exact diagnosis of his mental disabilities. He clearly is affected by some brain disease.

A key characteristic of Terry is that he is always ready to go somewhere. He has a backpack that he prepares with care each time before he leaves his room to go to the dining room. He takes enormous care in checking its contents before he decides that he is ready to go. He will put on a coat and a scarf before he hoists the backpack onto his back. When out of the room, he carefully closes the door behind him.

Terry always smiles when we are chatting.

Mina:	(I knock on the door which is ajar) Can I come in, Terry? (Terry does not answer, so I slowly push the door open and put my head round) Hello Terry, can I come in?
Terry:	Hello … … yes (Terry is sitting up on his bed, head against pillows, his jacket and neck scarf on, a magazine in his hands).
Mina:	How are you today, Terry?
Terry:	Yes … … okay thank you? … … … how are you?
Mina:	I am very well, thank you Terry …
Terry:	… yes …
Mina:	Can I sit down, Terry?
Terry:	Yes.
Mina:	What are you looking at, Terry?
Terry:	… this … … the magazine … yes …
Mina:	What sort of magazine, Terry?
Terry:	… (Terry lifts the magazine and looks at it intently) … these … airplanes … yes …
Mina:	Interesting … did you work with airplanes, Terry?
Terry:	Yes … … yes, I did … …
Mina:	Were you a pilot, Terry?
Terry:	Pilot? …
Mina:	Did you fly airplanes, Terry?
Terry:	(Terry looks at me intently … I can almost hear his brain ticking) fly airplanes?
Mina:	(I nod).
Terry:	No … I don't think so … no…
Mina:	What work did you do with airplanes, Terry? (Terry looks at me for quite some time, then he slowly gets off the bed, approaches his desk, sits on the chair by his desk and opens a drawer; he finds what he is looking for, takes it out and hands it to me to look at)

Terry:	This ...
Mina:	A photograph album?
Terry:	Yes (Terry smiles with pride in his eyes) ...
Mina:	Photographs of airplanes?
Terry:	Yes ...
Mina:	They're very nice photos, Terry ... they look professional.
Terry:	Yes ... (Terry turns pages to show me) ...
Mina:	Who took these photographs, Terry?
Terry:	... (Terry smiles) Yes ...
Mina:	Did you take these photographs?
Terry:	(Bigger, broader smile) yes ... yes ...
Mina:	They are brilliant photos, Terry ... ... is that what you did as a job? Were you a professional photographer?
Terry:	Yes ... ... not professional ... no ...
Mina:	Aaaah ... you were an amateur photographer...
Terry:	Yes (Big smile of approval) ...
Mina:	Now I get it ... apologies Terry, I am a bit slow sometimes ... now I get it ... you liked taking photographs of airplanes ...
Terry:	Yes, yes, I did ... . (Terry looks for something else in his desk drawers) and this ...
Mina:	Drawings? ... of airplanes?
Terry:	Yes ...
Mina:	You really liked airplanes then, Terry?
Terry:	Yes, yes I did ...
Mina:	I am impressed, Terry ... they look very good drawings to me ...
Terry:	Yes ...
Mina:	I am no good at either ... drawing or taking photographs ...

Terry:	(Terry smiles at me and nods)
Mina:	Right, Terry… it's nearly lunch time … would you like to go to the dining room now?
Terry:	Okay …
Mina:	Shall I go with you?
Terry:	Right … (Terry is suddenly quite brisk in his movements)
	(A routine follows: Terry spends a fair bit of time checking the contents of his rucksack; when he is satisfied that everything in it is what he wants or needs for his outing, he gets up and puts on his back; he checks that all his drawers are properly closed, that the light is off in his bathroom and the door fully closed; then slowly we leave his bedroom)
Mina:	Ready?
Terry:	Yes…
Mina:	Okay … let's go … you know the way, don't you, Terry?
Terry:	Oh yes …
	(In the dining room, Terry takes one of the vacant chairs, sits down and takes his cutlery out of his rucksack; he places each item carefully on the table)
Mina:	Perfect … okay, Terry? Are you comfortable here?
Terry:	Yes … thank you …
Mina:	Perfect … I will go now, Terry … I'll see you next week … is that okay?
Terry:	Yes (Terry smiles and nods)

Terry's core person

More than anything else, I see that Terry must have been a gentleman, with quiet politeness and a life-long child-like fascination with airoplanes. His other favourite occupation is looking at photographs of his grandsons on his desk. I am confident that this interpretation is accurate because his daughter, who gave me permission to publish, did not correct a single word in this conversation. She asked me to use her father's family name, Terry. I had initially anonymised him. I am grateful for the family's vote of confidence.

Conversation with Pam

Pam's world is her bed. I do not know how long she has been bed-bound, totally reliant on carers to give her a sense of the worth of her life. Judging from the photos in her room, and from messages left on her chest of drawers for the carers, she has a devoted family. She is unable to move in bed by herself and unable to feed herself. She can often be heard shouting from her bed one of two phrases: 'please help me' or 'mum, come and help me'. She sounds distressed, but actually she is not.

Pam is quite aware of her state of being and never talks about it. Her mind appears to have chosen a focus point – her mother – and rarely veers from that. One carer has learnt Pam's favourite song (which I cannot remember!) and she often sings it to her. Pam loves those moments. I get to know her a little when I assist her with her breakfast. From time to time, I visit her mid-morning. Our conversations are always on the same topic and quite short. Pam forgets what she says from one moment to the next, yet I sense that she must have had quite a sharp brain, which was probably never used to its full potential. I feel that she must have been an astute lady and a loving mother.

Mina: Good morning, Pam, how are you this morning?
Pam: I'm alright.
Mina: Are you ready for your breakfast?
Pam: Yes.

Mina:	I have brought you some porridge and a cup of tea.
Pam:	That's nice ... can I have tea first?
Mina:	Of course, Pam ... It's a bit hot ... just take a little sip first ... okay?
Pam:	Okay.
	(Pam drinks quite a bit of the tea from the beaker with which I assist her as she cannot hold it herself. I learn over time to know when she has had enough to drink and move the beaker away from her)
Mina:	Porridge now, Pam?
Pam:	Yes please.
	... ...
Mina:	... there you are Pam... ready for the next mouthful?
Pam:	Yes ... that's so nice ...
Mina:	Is it as you like it, Pam?
Pam:	Oh yes ... lovely ... just right ...
Mina:	It's not too hot?
Pam:	No, it's just right ...
Mina:	Good ... I'll tell the chef that you like her porridge ...
Pam:	... it's always good ...
	(We take our time. I don't like to rush Pam, and she does ask for some more if I slow down too much; in between mouthfuls, I chat about this and that)
Mina:	... I was looking at the photos on your wall Pam ... you've got two grandsons?
Pam:	... yeah ... I guess so ...
Mina:	How old are they?
Pam:	Oh ... I don't know ... how many photos can you see?
Mina:	Well, you have quite a few photos ... your family I'm guessing ... but I can only see two photos of two young boys ...

Pam:	That must be them then …
Mina:	What are their names?
Pam:	… … I don't know … can't remember …
Mina:	Not important, Pam … I'm just being nosy …
Pam:	(Pam turns her head towards the window) what's it like outside?
Mina:	Not too bad today, Pam … a bit cloudy … a very reluctant sun trying to show itself from behind the pale clouds … it's okay, not raining anyway … I don't like the rain…
Pam:	No … can I have some more tea?
Mina:	Of course … there is still a bit left in the beaker … it may have gone cold … you tell me if it's okay …
Pam:	(Pam takes a sip and releases the beaker from her mouth) … it's a bit cold …
Mina:	I'll go and get you a fresh cup, okay? Is that alright?
Pam:	Yes please
Mina:	Okay I'll be back soon … would you like more porridge as well?
Pam:	No, I've had enough porridge, thank you
Mina:	(I return with the tea) I've come back, Pam, with another cup of tea; would you like it?
Pam:	No, I've had enough … can I have a chocolate?
Mina:	Of course, Pam … which one … you have a few different chocolates here …
Pam:	The small round ones … they're over there … somewhere … over there …
Mina:	Oh yes … I got them … they're in a bag … they look nice …here's one … (Pam eats one) … another one, Pam?
Pam:	Yes please …

COME AND TALK WITH ME

Mina:	Another one?
Pam:	I've had enough now …
Mina:	Okay … are you comfortable?
Pam:	Yes, thank you.
Mina:	Okay, I'll go and help in the dining room now Pam … I'll come back later … after I've finished in the dining room … okay?
Pam:	Okay.
	(A few minutes later, we begin to hear Pam shout out … 'mum come and help me' … 'mum come and help me' … I pop in).
Mina:	Hello Pam, can I help you?
Pam:	No … I'm alright …
Mina:	Are you sure?
Pam:	Quite sure … what's it like outside?
Mina:	It's not too bad, Pam … it's clouded over now … there was a little sunshine before … it's gone now…
Pam:	It's gone now …
Mina:	Would you like anything Pam?
Pam:	No, thank you…
Mina:	Okay, I'll go now, and I'll be back in a few minutes and we can chat … if you'd like that?
Pam:	That'll be nice …
Mina:	Okay, bye for now … back in a few minutes …
Pam:	Okay …
	(I leave the room and immediately I hear… 'mum, come and help me' … in increasing decibels 'mum, come and help me' … I return to Pam's room)
Mina:	Pam, you're asking for your mum?
Pam:	Was I?
Mina:	Yes Pam, I heard you shout 'mum come and help me'

21

Pam: Oh …
Mina: Can I call your mum for you?
Pam: Can you?
Mina: Yes, I can … I can get the number from the office
Pam: But you can't…
Mina: Why not?
Pam: She's dead, isn't she? (in a tone that says 'surely you know that!')
         (I know Pam's mum is dead; Pam doesn't know that I know).
Mina: When did she die?
Pam: Can't remember …
Mina: What was she like, your mum?
Pam: Nice … she was very nice …
Mina: Did you like your mum?
Pam: Oh yes … (In spite of my presence, Pam takes up again her shouts for help from her mother) 'mum come and help me'
Mina: How do you think your mum can help you, Pam?
Pam: I don't know what she can do … she's dead, isn't she?
Mina: Do you think that she can help you from the other side?
Pam: Oh yes … she can …
Mina: I am glad … she sounds like a good mum …
Pam: Yeah … I'm tired now.
Mina: Alright Pam … I'll leave you now and come back another time … shall I?
Pam: Yes, please.

Pam's core person

Being with Pam is always a moving experience for me, each time. Pam's life has been severely reduced by her physical disabilities and, to a great degree, by her mind. And yet, I can feel that she has been a warm person and a loving daughter, above all else.

When I resume my visits to Redbond Lodge after the second COVID lockdown is lifted, I find that Pam's mental attention has a new focus. I enter her room, and she is talking softly to herself.

Pam: I love my daddy … I love my daddy.
Mina: Hello, Pam.
Pam: Hello.
Mina: How are you today, Pam?
Pam: I'm alright … I love my daddy … yes, I love my daddy … my daddy is a nice daddy … I love my daddy.
Mina: That's nice, Pam … that you loved your daddy …
Pam: Yes, I love my daddy … can I have a chocolate?
Mina: Of course … I'll just look for them because I can't see any right now …
Pam: Yes okay … I love my daddy …
Mina: I'm going to ask about your chocolates, Pam … I can't see any … I'll be back soon … okay?
Pam: Okay … I love my daddy.

Who could fail to be moved by such sounds? To have lived such a loving life as Pam must have done must be a wonderful bliss in which to relive one's memories.

Pam's family asked me to use her own name, which is Pam. I am privileged to give her, and them, the voice they deserve.

Conversation with Millie

M illie is in her late eighties. She is a good-looking woman. She is here because she suffered a stroke and she can no longer live by herself. She has one daughter who lives abroad and a son who lives somewhere in the South of England. She is fiercely proud of her children. She became a widow in her forties. She told me what work she had done in her life (which I have forgotten!) and much about her children and grandchildren and a new addition to the family, a great-grand-daughter.

Millie is extremely well spoken and very polite. She is a lady who knows how to say the right thing at the right time. She seems to be a person who is mentally strong, who believes that one should not be too critical of what others do and say in order not to upset things as they are. She does, however, expect a high standard of care, which she is very pleased to say, she gets at Redbond Lodge.

I get to know Millie quite well. We sit and chat in her room, where she feels most comfortable. A few months after arriving, she suffers another stroke, which leaves her in greater need of personal care and can no longer walk by herself to the dining room. She is pushed in a wheelchair so that she can enjoy the company of other residents at breakfast time and at other meal times. She can just about still use her right arm and hand to feed herself.

A hidden Millie begins to reveal herself in her frustration at not being able to do more for and by herself, without constant need of carers' assistance. A Millie that she has successfully controlled, with her principles of behaving in a socially appropriate way. Good manners are the axioms she had grown up with and that she has instilled in her children. She expects everybody to behave as per the same high social standards by which she conducts herself. As a result, in her unfamiliar state of total dependency, she often lashes out, both verbally and physically, at the carers, if she is in an angry and helpless mood.

Some mornings at breakfast, Millie is forlorn, sad, resentful and so unhappy after she has suffered this second stroke. On other mornings, she is radiant. One morning, I approach her at her table:

Mina: Good morning, Millie, how are you today?

Millie: (Smiles) I am very well, thank you; are you well this morning?

Mina: Yes, I am Millie; it's a beautiful morning outside.

Millie: Oh yes, I can see that, but it's also a bit cold, isn't it?

Mina: Yes, it is; a bright sunny and crisp winter Friday morning, Millie.

Millie: Yes, I could feel it this morning in my room; I like the window open.

Mina: Now, Millie, have you had enough to eat?

Millie: Yes, thank you; maybe a bit of toast? But can I tell you a secret first?

Mina: Of course, but can you trust me with your secret?

Millie: I think so.

Mina: Go on then, what is it?

Millie: I'm going to whisper it…I've just had a baby (a radiant smile on Millie's face).

Mina:	Well congratulations Millie! Are you happy with that?
Millie:	Oh yes, I am ever so happy!
Mina:	And how are you feeling?
Millie:	Oh, very well! I am forty you know!
Mina:	That's okay; my mum was forty-two when my youngest sister was born; it's alright.
Millie:	Yes…. (Millie continues to smile).
Mina:	Is the baby okay?
Millie:	Oh yes… (Millie continues to smile).
Mina:	Now, shall I get your toast Millie?
Millie:	Yes, please (Millie gestures how she wants it cut).
Mina:	I think I remember how you like it Millie, cut up in four little triangles (I make appropriate gestures).
Millie:	Yes, thank you.
Mina:	And you like it with jam, don't you? Or would like to have a change today and have it with marmalade?
Millie:	With jam, thank you.
Mina:	Okay, I'll go and get it; I'll be back in a minute.

A fusion of time and space

In this short exchange with Millie, I aim to capitalise on her happy mood and help her to feel good about herself. Millie's mind has taken her to a moment in her life when she must have experienced immense joy at the birth of her baby. Maybe she had been forty, maybe she had not. Does it matter? No.

At that moment, which to me is the present in 2019, Millie's moment resides in her past, more than forty years in her previous life, but has presented itself to her mind as her actual present. It is a moment to remember and cherish. It is a moment in which her mind has temporarily put aside her older body's failure to hang on to her physical independence. It is a moment of intense reality for Millie. I see it in her eyes and in her beautiful smile. She remains contented for the rest of her breakfast time. Her present lies in her past. Her future is a foreign country for which she is no longer able to plan.

Millie is an anonymised name. I am happy to respect the family's wishes that I keep using this name. I thank them for permission to publish this conversation.

.

SECTION TWO:
CONVERSATIONS WITH MY MOTHER ANGELA

My mother was diagnosed with vascular dementia in her mid-seventies. As her mental and physical skills deteriorated over the months and years, I noticed that she never stopped being determined and single-minded, stubborn and argumentative. She never ceased wanting to fulfil her role as a mother and wife whose responsibilities were to take care of the people in her life. She remained true to herself – the same person – until she died.

Conversations with my mother Angela

My mother, Angela, was mentally strong, determined and single-minded. At times, she could come across as opinionated, stubborn and argumentative. She was also devoted to her role as a carer and protector of her young family, her husband and her mother, until her mother died. She had an amazing ability of recalling the minutest details of encounters and conversations.

In the memoir that I wrote about these years of my mother's life,[6] I talked about how she never stopped being the person that she had always been and how her potent memory skills would manifest themselves in what I called 'a fusion of time and space'.

These conversations are extracts from that memoir. Some took place in the residential care home where Angela went to live in the last four years of her life.

The first conversation below took place in the care home. My sister Lucia and I used to take our mother out on a Saturday to enjoy her company and also to give her a day out of the nursing home. We would go to Carsington Water in Derbyshire or to a garden centre or to Arkwright's Cromford Mills or to Chatsworth

---

6   *Thank you lady* published in 2017 by Austin Macauley and available on Amazon.

House to enjoy the graceful undulations of the Derbyshire hills. These outings would always include lunch, which were mostly very enjoyable events: a mother and two daughters in relaxed companionship. Occasionally Angela was not in a good mood and lunch would be fraught with controlled anxiety. On the occasion of this particular conversation Angela was relaxed, smiling, loving, interested in her daughters' current life.

Lucia: Hello, mum.
Angela: Hi, Lucia.
            (Mother and daughter smiled at each other. They had the same warm and affectionate smile).
Lucia: How are you today, mum?
Angela: I am fine... and your children?
Lucia: My children? ... they're ok.
Angela: Who's looking after them today?
Lucia: No one, mum.
Angela: Are they at school?
Lucia: No mum ... (Lucia laughed, Angela smiled ... somewhat confused) ... They've grown up!
Angela: Yes ... of course ... (still looking confused).
Lucia: John has gone to a football match.
Angela: So, he plays football then?
Lucia: No mum ... he's gone to see a football match ... (Lucia maintained eye contact with her mother; she could see that her mother was having difficulty connecting with the past in her mind with the news of the present in her daughter's life; she kept smiling at her mother.)
Lucia: They've grown up mum ... just like I have!
Angela: Well ... you never grow up! (They laughed together)

Lucia:	And Richard is in Australia …
Angela:	Why? … Isn't that a long way away?
Lucia:	Yes mum, it's a long way away.
Angela:	Well, we all have our destiny.
Lucia:	You're right, mum … My destiny is to remain for ever young … (Lucia teased her mum).
Angela:	Well … if you have grown-up children, you too will get old!
Lucia:	But not yet?
Angela:	No, not yet!

Fusion of time and space

This is an example of what I call a *fusion of time and space*. Angela knew that her daughter in front of her at this moment has two children, but in her mind's eye she sees her two small grandsons. In her mind's eye, there are no intervening years from when they were little children to now when they are grown up.

On another occasion, Angela appeared to be much more in tune with the 'present' reality of her daughters' lives. Lucia and I were sitting with her in her room, waiting for a carer to prepare mum for our Saturday outing. When she was calm, she seemed to be mentally 'in the moment', a moment that encompassed the entire lives of her two daughters. She seemed to recall that their sons were grown-up men.

Angela:	And, Jonathan … what's he doing now? (asking me, her eldest daughter).
Mina:	Mum, he's got his own production company … he makes short films …
Angela:	How lovely (smiling with grandmotherly pride in her

eyes) ... and Richard? (turning to Lucia) ... where is he now? (appearing to remember that he had been somewhere).

Lucia: He's back in England, mum; he's got a job with a science publication; he's an editor.

Angela: ... Aaah! ... (exclaiming as if she was completely au fait with what that meant).

Lucia: And John works as a graphic designer.

Angela: They are all so clever ... you have done very well with your children ... and they are all in England?

Lucia: Yes mum, they are all here in England.

Angela: Good ... it's not so bad here.

Lucia: So, mum, you have never regretted bringing us here? ... to this blessed land, as you like to say?

Angela: No ... (laughing) ... this blessed land.

Indeed, Angela loved England and the life that she and her husband had built in their adopted country. She had come to England at the age of forty, with five children ranging in age from six to seventeen. Her sixth child was born in England when she was forty-two years old. She had lived half her life in Italy.

She always said that she had never regretted leaving Italy, but she thought constantly about the people she had grown up with and the life she had lived in Gioia del Colle, her Italian hometown. When she was so engrossed in some activity or other that she forgot her surroundings and where she was, we, her children, could tell from the expressions on her face that she was thinking of some event that might have taken place in Italy at some point in the distant past. We would tease her and beg her to tell us where she had been, with her wandering mind.

Sometimes she would smile and at other times she would cry, depending on the images that had invaded her mind. She would always start her responses with 'eh beh...' ... 'ah, well...' and she would give us vivid accounts of her mind's meanderings as if she were experiencing them in the moment, and no years or country frontiers had intervened in the process of her life. The stories sounded as if non-essential details – such as the death of a person – were immaterial to the core memory.

This 'panoramic landscape' of her mental life would present itself in her conversations during her 'dementia' years, much to the consternations of those with whom she was talking. One episode was particularly illustrative of this mental hopping between the Italian life of her first forty years and the English life since coming to live in England.

The following conversations took place during the early years of mum's 'dementia'. She had not yet gone to live in the care home. My father's sister-in-law Teresa (wife of his younger brother Rocco) had come to visit from Italy with her son Pino.

Angela:	Why didn't Rocco come?
Teresa:	Oh, Lina ... Rocco is no longer with us ... he died ...
Angela:	He's dead? ... When? ... Why didn't you tell us?
Teresa:	Yes, Lina, you did know (Angela was known as 'Lina' in Italy ... from Angela's diminutive Angelina) ... don't you remember, Peppino (my father's Italian name) came to Italy to see him just the week before he died?
Angela:	No, I didn't know ... he didn't tell me anything ...
Teresa:	Yes, Lina, he did tell you ... he wouldn't have come without your knowledge.

Angela: Well … yes … perhaps … and your children, how are they?
Teresa: The children? … don't you remember? … they have their own children … have you not seen that Pino is here with me? … He's in the garden … with Peppino … your husband …
Angela: … of course … (rubbing the ridge of her nose … a gesture that Angela used when she couldn't quite figure out what was going on).

The day after this conversation, Teresa returned to Angela's house from an outing. Angela greeted her warmly.

Angela: Hello Teresa, when did you arrive?
Teresa: Just now … we went to visit the castle at Nottingham.
Angela: In Nottingham? … But …
Teresa: Yes … Mimmo took us …
Angela: But Rocco and the children?
Teresa: Oh no, Rocco is no longer with us … but Pino is here with us … Ginetta couldn't come.
Angela: And how long will you stay?
Teresa: Two more days … we came yesterday and we're going back the day after tomorrow.
Angela: You came yesterday? … and where did you stay?
Teresa: Here … with you.
Angela: Aaaah …. (she was not sure whether Teresa was right but appeared to have decided to go along with her explanation).

That evening at the dinner table, the conversation centred around family reminiscences during which Pino wanted to know from his uncle for what wartime action he had received the medal hanging on the wall from the Italian government. At the end of Peppino's account, which Angela had been following without interrupting, she exclaimed:

Angela: Yes, the war! ... it is because of the war that we came to this country!
Peppino: Come on, don't say stupid things ... what do you mean the war? ...
Angela: Yes ... it was the war ... I know ... (looking confused) ... I know ...
Antonella: (Their daughter understands what her mother is trying to say) Mum is trying to say that her brother was already here ...
Peppino: Ah, yes ... but that's another story ...
Angela: What other story? ... It's the same story ... If it hadn't been for my brother ... we would never have come here ....
Peppino: You're right ... but they know that story ...
Teresa: Yes Lina ... you have told us that story lots of times ...
Angela: No, I never told you.

Often, this 'fusion of time and space' would manifest itself in mum's recalling of her life. In this short conversation, in the care home, Angela was talking to her husband Peppino about her mother who had died many years ago (when Angela was about thirty-six years old) as if she were still alive and she herself was an unmarried daughter:

Peppino: Don't you want to eat?

Angela: I don't want any … and you, where have you been?
Peppino: Here … I've been here … you were sleeping? …
Angela: I must go home … mum is waiting for me …
Peppino: Your mother? … where is she, your mother?
Angela: At home … she is waiting for me … she's got dinner ready … I must go home.
Peppino: Which home?
Angela: What do you mean? … home, my house.
Peppino: Your house is here.
Angela: Here? … what do you mean here?
Peppino: To which house do you want to go? Ripley?
Angela: (looking at her husband, confused) … yes, here, in Ripley.
Peppino: Okay, we'll go home after you have eaten.
Angela: I said no … that's enough … I want to go home.
Peppino: For now, we stay here … go on, eat something.
Angela: I said I don't want to eat … okay? Enough … don't make me angry … mum is waiting for me.
Peppino: Your poor mother … does she know that you are here?
Angela: Yes, she does … call her … tell her that I'm on my way.
Peppino: Alright then … I'll tell her.

Angela would often display anger and frustration with her destiny and vent her disappointments to anyone who was in the vicinity at that particular moment. This aspect of her character was accentuated in the years lived in the residential care home, when she would quietly shout out 'I don't deserve this'. On one occasion, I found her very angry and agitated. She and another resident had been shouting at each another:

Mina:	Mum, whom are you shouting at?
Angela:	Oh, Giacomina (my full name).
Mina:	Why are you angry?
Angela:	Why … why … give me a hand …
Mina:	Do you want to go to the toilet?
Angela:	No, let me stand up (she shouted).
Mina:	Mum, you can't … wait, I'll call a carer.
Angela:	I don't need a carer… what are you talking about? I'll do it myself (she tried to shuffle herself in the chair, pushing her arms into the armrests, finding strength in her anger. When she couldn't anymore, she collapsed back sobbing) … I didn't deserve this.
Mina:	I know, mum.
Angela:	What do you know? … Go away … go away …

The same person

More than anything, mum never lost her sense of the main role in her life that she had always taken very seriously: making sure that she had prepared a good meal for her husband when he came home from a hard day on a building site. He would have spent the day working his bones to the ground to give his family a decent living. The least she could do for him in return was to ensure that a good plate of pasta was waiting for him on his homecoming. Poignantly, this was her obsession even when she did not recognise her husband at the very moment that all she wanted in the world was to go home and have dinner with him at their dinner table:

| Angela: | (Peppino was sitting at the dinner table with Angela in the care home. A carer had asked |

Angela if she would like some dinner) ... no, thank you, lady.

Peppino: Come on, eat a little.

Angela: No.

Peppino: Come on, you must eat something ... try a little meat? ... it looks good.

Angela: I said no ... I already prepared dinner.

Peppino: What do you mean ... you've prepared dinner?

Angela: It's all on the table ... we'll eat together ... with my husband.

Peppino: Come on ... this is your dinner.

Angela: No, stop ... I said no.

Peppino: Would you like some grapes?

Angela: I said no.
(She pushed his hand away. The grapes rolled on to the floor. He bent down to pick them up. She looked down at him. Her eyes veiled over. Why can't this man leave her alone? Her husband would come soon. Where was he? What was he doing here ... this man?).

Peppino: What is it? (he asked gently).

Angela: (She made a 'what-do-you-care' gesture) ... and my husband? ... Where is he?

Peppino: He will come ... he will come ...

A continuous present
Angela was her very own self. With her brain damaged by disconnected airwaves, her life became a panoramic single camera shot, with no past or present and definitely no future. It was at times an amazing experience listening to her flitting from

one event to another as if they were all and the same. Only she knew the thread that connected them. We were witnessing a collage of a life that we could only see as a mirage. It was quite wonderous.

SECTION THREE:
INCIDENTAL CONVERSATIONS AT REDBOND LODGE

Sometimes conversations are designed to achieve a particular aim: find out what might be upsetting a person or seek an answer to an uncharacteristic behaviour.

At other times, conversations are a natural progression from a 'hello, how are you'. Often, they are a cry for help.

Here are a few such 'incidental' conversations. Incidental because they are not the result of a planned visit and only occurred the once.

I remember them clearly because of their unusual context and because of the strength of the communication that made an impact on me.

Incidental conversation with Rose

One day I was asked by one of the managers at the care home if I would sit with one particular resident for a few minutes and see if I could get some verbal response from her. Apparently, she had had another stroke recently and her family was not able to communicate with her. The family was quite distressed.

I had often said hello to this lady and asked a 'how are you today?' at breakfast time, but I had not actually visited her. This was a long time ago and I cannot remember her name, so I'll call her Rose.

I can still see her in my mind and hear her voice. She is physically very infirm. She sits in a very high chair propped up with cushions, her legs stretched out onto a chair extension for leg support. Her right arm has some mobility, and she taps her fingers on the table-extension in front of her.

Mina: Hello Rose ... how are you?
Rose: (Rose looks at me with bright eyes).
Mina: I am Mina ... we've met before, Rose ... can I sit with you for a few minutes?
Rose: Yes, I remember.
Mina: How are you today?
Rose: ... Yes ... I am okay ... how are you?

Mina:	I am good thank you Rose … are you tapping a tune on your table?
Rose:	… (Rose looks at me … her fingers stop for a second, then they start tapping again).
Mina:	(With a smile on my face, I try to imitate Rose's tapping) … what do you think, Rose? … I am not as good as you are?
Rose:	(Rose smiles and continues to tap with the same tempo)
Mina:	Do you play the piano, Rose?
Rose:	… I used to … not any more …
Mina:	I can't play any instrument … I had to learn to read music when I was at school in Italy … but I cannot remember it at all.
Rose:	… … no … it's hard …
Mina:	Can you read music, Rose?
Rose:	Oh yes …
Mina:	What other instruments can you play, Rose?
Rose:	… … no … just the piano …
Mina:	And you sing too, Rose?
Rose:	… not anymore … … .
Mina:	What kind of music do you like, Rose?
Rose:	… … all sorts really … …
Mina:	Which do you sing though? … folk music? Or … jazz type? … like Edith Piaf maybe? …
Rose:	No nothing like that … … (Rose smiles) …
Mina:	Classical maybe? …
Rose:	Yes, classical …
Mina:	Did you sing in concerts, Rose?
Rose:	… … oh no … nothing like that …
Mina:	You are looking tired, Rose … would you like to rest?

Rose: Yes … I think so …
Mina: Okay Rose … I'll see you another time?
          (Rose nods and I leave her to doze as she closes
          her eyes).

This conversation took about twenty to thirty minutes. I reported to the manager that Rose was able to communicate after this second stroke if given time to take in the question and process it in her mind. It also helped to pick up on some activity or gesture initiated by Rose – in this case I copied her finger tapping on the table. I also prompted Rose by asking her questions related to tapping and building up on her responses. For example, if she had said that she didn't play the piano, I might have asked about tap-dancing, or computer work or anything else that might have come to mind. It was essential to pick up her cues and give her prompts, which she could use in thinking her answers to my questions.

Incidental conversation
with Cynthia

There are often visiting entertainers at Redbond Lodge Care Home: musicians, magicians, dogs and goats ... occasionally a pet goat or two, yes. On this particular morning (at time of writing after release of lockdown), it is a singer with a repertoire of popular songs from the 1950s and 1960s, appropriate to the young days of the residents in the home at the time of my visits, between 2016 and 2021. As I walk around chatting to the assembled audience, waiting for the show to start, this lady of a cheerful disposition takes my hand to tell me something. I have not met her before, and I do not know her name. I will call her Cynthia.

Cynthia: Hello dear ... do you know ... I used to teach all these here ...
Mina: How wonderful!
Cynthia: Yes, all of them ... well, maybe not all of them ...
Mina: Were you a primary or secondary teacher ...
Cynthia: Ah ... that's a question ... I don't think I can remember ...
Mina: I was a teacher too ...
Cynthia: Were you? ...
Mina: Yes ... secondary teacher ... I loved it ...

Cynthia: Oh, I too ... oh yes ... all of these here ... I used to teach them ...

Mina: Where did you teach, Cynthia?

Cynthia: Oh ... around ... do you know, I can't remember?

Mina: Well, it's not important ... I am just nosy!

Cynthia: (Cynthia laughs) ... anyway, what's going on ... why are we sitting here?

Mina: Ah ... good question ... I believe we are waiting for an entertainer ...

Cynthia: A what? Sounds ...

Mina: A singer I think ... someone to sing to us ...

Cynthia: That's nice ... Is it? ... What do you think?

Mina: It could be fun? ... e-n-t-e-r-t-a-i-n-i-n-g... what do you think?

Cynthia: (Cynthia laughs a lot) ... oh you are funny! ... but you know, it is funny to see them all ... I used to teach them, you know? Yes ...

Mina: So, you remember your students?

Cynthia: ... oh yes ... well not all of them ... but some you don't forget, do you?

Mina: Which school did you teach in?

Cynthia: Here in Dunmow ...

Mina: Dunmow Primary School?

Cynthia: Ah, now you're asking me ... you know, I can't remember ... not at first ...but yes that one as well ...

Mina: Well, here is the entertainer ... let's hope he can sing!

Cynthia: Ooooh .... (Cynthia laughs) ...

Mina: I'll see you in a minute, Cynthia ...

Cynthia: Yes, okay dear ... (Cynthia lets go of my hand).

Cynthia is very articulate. She displays the fusion of time and place that I first noticed in my mother many years ago, a phenomenon that presents a life's events as a continuous canvas. It brings to mind the Bayeux Tapestry: a long canvas illustration of events that led to the Battle of Hastings in 1066. You can go backwards and forwards looking at these events as you walk along the wall taking in the series of events until they begin to overlap with one another in your mind as you try to remember their sequence as they happened. Cynthia knows she had been a teacher who had loved her job but could not demarcate whom she taught when and where.

Incidental conversation
with Donald

B efore COVID, I pay a brief visit in the unit at Redbond Lodge where residents with greater mental and physical needs live. The unit has an open plan sitting room-cum-dining-room. It is nearly lunch time. I stop to chat with a very well-dressed gentleman who is a recent arrival. I only see him this one time. I do not remember his name. I will call him Donald.

Mina: Good morning sir, how are you today?
Donald: Good morning … yes, I am okay … well I think I am … yes good …
Mina: I have not met you before now … when did you arrive?
Donald: Only yesterday … I think … yes anyway, not long ago … I am here for a respite … a few days …
Mina: Where do you live?
Donald: Not far from here … …. Who are you?
Mina: Oh, I'm sorry, how rude of me … I am Mina, I am a visitor …
Donald: You visit here?
Mina: Yes … and you are?
Donald: Donald … Donald … yes, I don't know why I am

here really ... it's all very strange ... she went off ...
(Donald shrugs his shoulders) ... so here I am ...

Mina: She?

Donald: Yes, she ... there is nothing I can do ... well all I can
say ... he's alright really ... nothing wrong with him
... I don't mind him ... he's a decent bloke ...

Mina: Are you married, Donald?

Donald: Hmm? ... yes, well I was ... not anymore ...

Mina: Where does your wife live?

Donald: She died ... oh, a while ago ... I can't remember
exactly ... ... now here I am ... waiting ...

Mina: Where do you plan to go?

Donald: I am not too sure ... somewhere ... I came for respite
you see; my son is looking ... my house ... but anyway ... I don't mind ... I have nothing against him ...
he's a nice bloke ... there you go ... (Donald shrugs
his shoulders).

Mina: Where is your house, Donald?

Donald: Not far from here.

Mina: Anyway, how do you like it here, in the meantime?

Donald: It's okay ... yes ... it's fine ...

Mina: I am pleased ... people okay here?

Donald: Yes, it's fine.
(Lunch arrives for Donald and his co-residents)

Mina: Right, I must go now, Donald, your lunch is here ...
good chatting with you ... I'll probably pop in next
week if that's okay?

Donald: Yes okay ...

Mina: Bye for now.

Donald: Yes bye.

I never saw Donald again. He showed a resigned stoicism which appeared to be a core characteristic of his. I imagine that he had always been a gentleman who respected people's wishes to do as they chose, though he might have been hurt by their actions.

Incidental conversation with Susan

I stop and chat with Susan just the once, though I see her a few times sitting in the reception area of Redbond Lodge, immersed in telephone conversations. I do not know her name. She reminds me of a Susan I used to know, so I think of her as Susan. I stop to chat with her one day because she seems agitated as she comes off the phone. I do not know her condition. She talks very fast. Possibly because she is so upset. Or maybe that is the way she always talks. I show this by not using any punctuation in her utterances in this brief conversation. She is not there when I resume my visits after the first lockdown,

Mina: Are you okay?
Susan: No not really
Mina: You seem quite upset.
Susan: I am yes I am I don't know what's happening I keep asking and I am only supposed to be here while they sell my house, I'm moving in a new flat and now they tell me it's not ready.
Mina: The flat is not ready?
Susan: I don't know I am getting different stories I keep asking I have no idea what's happening you see I am only here until my house is sold.
Mina: Who is doing this for you?
Susan: My daughter is I really don't know why I couldn't do

54

it myself they said it's for the best and I agreed now I'm stuck in here and I can't do anything and they won't give me a straight answer.

Mina: I am sorry to hear all this; it's upsetting for you; I can see that.

Susan: Well, I'm getting quite worried now I agreed to come here just while they sort it out, they're waiting to sell my house and I'm still here.

Mina: How are you finding this place, anyway?

Susan: It's alright I don't mind it for a while but I shouldn't be here this long I'm really quite annoyed now they've sold my house.

Mina: Did you agree to selling your house?

Susan: I guess so yes, I did it's too big anyway I didn't want to sell it, but my daughter said it's for the best.

Mina: Where is your new flat?

Susan: Near my daughter I think I am not so sure there's nothing I can do from here and they don't give me a straight answer so I don't know I don't know how long I've got to stay here and I'm quite annoyed yes fed up.

Mina: Can I help you in any way?

Susan: Oh dear no thanks you you've kind everybody is very kind here I just need to sort this out sorry dear I've got to take this call.

Mina: (I left Susan to take her call, which she did while walking away. That was my last glimpse of Susan as she went towards the lift, presumably to return to her quarters).

SECTION FOUR:
CONVERSATIONS WITH KATH AND EVIE AT REDBOND LODGE

I got to know Kath and Evie very well over a period of years. They did not know each other, but I have a feeling they would have become friends had they been able to meet and spend time together.

Neither had a brain disease.

Both had sharp minds.

Each lady had a wonderful spirit towards her fellow humans. I learnt much from their stoicism and dignity.

Conversation with Kath

To me, Kath personifies true, honest dignity: she is candid about her body weaknesses and does not hide behind the veil of modesty. In addition, she has a degree of self-awareness rarely seen in any human being. She is given to mental self-flagellation and lives with a continual sense that she could have been a better person. Yet she is entertaining and has an avid interest in world affairs. She is realistic about the limitations of the care and attention she can expect in a large, residential care home, with well-intentioned yet, occasionally, thoughtless carers. She is not shy about voicing her opinions if she feels undeservedly patronised.

Mina: (The first time I visit Kath, she is lying in her bed in her darkened room. Her bedroom door is open, so I approach her bed silently in case she is asleep. She senses my presence and opens her eyes).

Kath: Oh hello …

Mina: Hello, Kath … how are you?

Kath: Who are you?

Mina: I am Mina, a volunteer visitor … how are you this morning?

Kath: Not so good … what time is it?

Mina: It's about 11.00 … have you had any breakfast?

Kath: No, I didn't feel like it … I don't want anything …

Mina:	Can I stay with you for a while ...?
Kath:	Yes, okay ... can you open the curtains a bit ... what's it like outside?
Mina:	It's beautiful weather, Kath ... shall I open the window to get some fresh air in?
Kath:	Yes, okay.... I need to go to the toilet ... I'm afraid I'm not in a good way ...
Mina:	Shall I go and find a carer, Kath .... Do you need a carer or can you manage on your own?
Kath:	I think I need a carer, yes ... can you call one for me?
Mina:	(A carer comes to assist Kath) right, Kath, I'll wait outside in the corridor; I'll come back in when you're ready ... if you'd like that?
Kath:	Yes, okay.
Mina:	(I go back into Kath's room when the carer leaves. Kath is dressed and sitting in her chair).
Kath:	Hello again, who did you say you are?
Mina:	I am a volunteer visitor, Kath. I come in a couple of times a week. I have been a few times ... popped into your room, but each time you were asleep ... or looked asleep ...
Kath:	Oh well, sometimes I just don't feel like getting up ... I'm a miserable so-and-so ... (Kath chuckles) ... there's not much to do here ... except think ...
Mina:	What do you think about?
Kath:	I'm always depressed ... I am a miserably depressed person, I am ... (self—deprecating chuckles) ... I can't help it ...
Mina:	What makes you miserable and depressed, Kath?
Kath:	Everything ... ... all my life I've been depressed ... more or less ...

Mina: How was your life when you were growing up?

Kath: It was alright ... you know ... village life ...

Mina: How did you get on with your parents?

Kath: It was good ... oh yes ... it was later ... I should have helped more ... but I couldn't help it ...

Mina: What did your father do for work, Kath?

Kath: He was a game keeper ... he loved his job ... we lived in a nice cottage ... yes in the country ...

Mina: It sounds as if you had an idyllic childhood ....

Kath: Oh yes ... we did ...

Mina: ... did you have any brothers or sisters?

Kath: One brother ... he was really good ... very bright ...

Mina: How did you get on with him?

Kath: Oh, very close ... he was a very good man ... my niece comes to see me every Sunday ...

Mina: Your brother's daughter? Does she live around Dunmow?

Kath: Yes ... she thought I'd be better here ... I had carers, three times a day ... but I got to the point where I couldn't look after myself anymore ... so here I am? (Kath chuckles).

Mina: How is your life here?

Kath: It's alright ... people are busy ... you can't always get a response when you want it ... especially at night ... you ring the buzzer ... and you wait ... and then ... well, you end up (Kath lifts her shoulders, as if to say ...'you know what I mean') ... I can't help it ...

Mina: I am sorry to hear that, Kath... would you like me to mention this in the office?

Kath: You can do if you want ... but it won't do any good ... I know they're busy ... there's so many people ....

Mina: Well, I'll mention it anyway ... they can have a word with the night manager ...

Kath: But tell me about yourself ... it's good to meet a new person ...

Mina: My name is Mina ... I am a volunteer visitor ... I come a couple of times a week .... I have two grand-children ...

Kath: What are their names ...

Mina: Daisy and Jay ... they live in Peckham, in London ... do you know it?

Kath: I know of it ... I've never been ... from that TV pro-gramme ... what was it called?

Mina: I don't know ... I only know of one, which I very oc-casionally watched, comedy ... with David Jason? Can't remember the name ...

Kath: I know ... only fools and horses ... that was it!

Mina: I think you are right, Kath ... and you, where did you live before coming here, Kath?

Kath: Up in Leicestershire ... in (I can't remember the name of the place Kath said) ... do you know it?

Mina: No, I don't ... but not far from Derbyshire ... that's where my family lives, most of them anyway ...

Kath: Whereabout?

Mina: Ripley ... not far from Nottingham and Derby.

Kath: Yes ... it's beautiful countryside up there ... I like where we lived ...

Mina: Did you live there all your life?

Kath: Yes ... I did ... I guess that's boring ...

Mina: Why would it be boring .... If you were happy there ...

Kath: I was ... then my father got ill ... and I couldn't look after him ... that's what I get depressed about ...

Mina:	What happened?
Kath:	It was horrible ... I couldn't face it ...
Mina:	Did he have an accident?
Kath:	No, he had bowel cancer .... I couldn't face it .... And I feel guilty about that ... I should have been kinder ....
Mina:	Maybe it's time to be kinder to yourself, Kath ... was there anything more you could have done for him than you did?
Kath:	No, I don't think so ... but I should not have hated doing it so much ...
Mina:	Have you told your niece how you feel about this?
Kath:	Maybe I should ... (Kath laughs) ... she's almost a vicar ...
Mina:	Is she?
Kath:	No ... but she could be ... she teaches ... somewhere ... at a university ... near here ... that's why I moved here so that she doesn't have to travel up to Leicestershire to see me ... she's very busy with the church ... she's so good ... not like me (another chuckle ... Kath laughs at herself easily).
Mina:	Are you contented with your life here, Kath?
Kath:	It could be worse, I guess; there's always somebody worse than you ...anyway, it's good to talk to you ... I'm sorry I go on about my misery ...
Mina:	No need to apologise, Kath ... we all get down sometimes ....Anyhow, I have to go now; can I come again?
Kath:	That would be very nice ... it's good to talk to someone new ... you take care ...

Kath is a very good conversationalist. We rarely talk about the same things. We sometimes talk for an hour or more. Her family, her niece and her nephew and his family, mean a great deal to her and enjoys telling me how wonderful they are to her. They are her favourite subject of conversation.

Kath: There you are (as I walked into Kath's room I am greeted with a big smile and expectation) ... I must tell you about T (a young male carer whose name I have forgotten) and L (his girlfriend) ... you know they are leaving ...

Mina: No, I didn't know ...

Kath: They've got new jobs ... oh yes ...

Mina: I didn't know they were a couple.

Kath: Didn't you? They're my favourite ... I am really sad they're going ... but I'm happy for them ... I'll miss them ...

Mina: That's a shame ... there are other carers you're happy with, aren't there?

Kath: Oh yes ... (she laughs) ... there's some really good ones ... anyway ... what do you think of Trump then?

Mina: Why, what's he been up to now?

Kath: Oh, I don't know ... it would be funny if it wasn't so tragic ... he's hopeless ...

Mina: What I don't understand Kath, along with the rest of the world ... how come so many Americans voted for him?

Kath: Well, he's got something ....

Mina: What?

Kath: God knows, but something they like about him ... maybe they're all like him ... those that voted for him ... just Americans ... that don't care for other people ...

Mina: You could be right ...

Kath: ... let's just hope he doesn't push the button ...

Mina:	No! let's hope … anyhow, what about you this morning, how are you?
Kath:	I'm fine … tell me about the children … how are they?
Mina:	Do you want to see some photos? (We spend some time looking at my grandchildren's photos and little videos on my phone).
Kath:	I didn't see my nephew this last weekend … they're away skiing … in France I believe …
Mina:	You missed them?
Kath:	Oh yes, but they need a break. They are so good to me. I don't know what I would do without them. Did I tell you his daughter, the younger one, she just graduated, in nursing… she is so happy. And she's got herself a good job. Just what she wanted.
Mina:	You have a good family, Kath.
Kath	They are wonderful. Yes.

Kath's family was delighted to give me permission to publish these conversations with Kath. This is what her nephew Michael said in his email:

'..... what a wonderful idea. The most precious gift you can give is your time, and I know Kath really enjoyed every moment you spent with her. She always told us about the conversations you had with her. My sister and me are very happy for you to share your stories about Kath using her name (which is Kath with a "K")'

Conversation with Evie
– A speck of dust

I f it is possible to combine humility with dignity and pride, Evie personifies it. When I meet her, Evie has lived in Redbond Lodge for about five years. Her bed has been her 'home' for the latter part of those five years. This is our first conversation:

Mina: Hello Evie, can I sit with you for a while?
Evie: Hello dear, yes please.
Mina: How are you?
Evie: Who are you dear?
Mina: I am Mina. I am a volunteer visitor. Would you like me to visit you?
Evie: That would be very nice. What is your name?
Mina: It's Mina, Evie.
Evie: Nina, that's a nice name.
Mina: How are you feeling today, Evie?
Evie: Not so bad dear. I get a bit lonely. Everybody is so busy. But I'm alright.
Mina: How long have you lived here, Evie?
Evie: Oh, it's five years now.
Mina: That's quite a long time. What brought you here?
Evie: My husband came first … then I followed him … (a chuckle from Evie)

COME AND TALK WITH ME

Mina:	That must have been good … being together …
Evie:	He had Alzheimer's … but I could visit him …
Mina:	Where does he live now?
Evie:	In that cupboard … (Evie points to a cupboard) …
Mina:	In the cupboard? … The cream-coloured cupboard?
Evie:	Yes, that's the one.
Mina:	In the cupboard?
Evie:	Yes … I haven't seen him for a long time … I would like to touch him again …
Mina:	… Evie … tell me how he's in the cupboard …
Evie:	In a green container ….
Mina:	Would you like me to get it for you?
Evie:	Would you?
Mina:	Of course, …. (I go to the cupboard and take out a bottle green urn … I realise with certainly now that this urn contains the ashes of her husband; I take it to Evie). There you are Evie …
Evie:	Hello, my darling … oh my darling …. How are you?
Mina:	(I sit in silence for quite some time).
Evie:	Can you lift him up for me dear?
Mina:	Of course, Evie (I lift the urn up to Evie's lip; she kisses the urn and caresses it gently).
Evie:	Bye my darling … see you very soon I hope … you can put him back now …
Mina:	Are you sure, Evie?
Evie:	Yes, I am sure … thank you …
Mina:	(Evie has a calm, gentle smile; her eyes follow me as I replace the urn of her husband's ashes to its place). How long were you married for, Evie … before he died?
Evie:	Oh, a very long time … I can't remember …

Mina: How old were you when you married?

Evie: Oh, I think I was about 20? Or 19? ... I can't remember exactly ...

Mina: I get the feeling that yours was a very happy marriage, Evie.

Evie: Oh yes it was ... well we had our moments ... (Evie chuckles) ... he was a lovely husband ... caring ... yes ...

Mina: You are looking tired now ... shall I leave you to rest?

Evie: That would be nice dear ... yes, I am tired a little ... will you come again?

Mina: I would love to do that ... next time I come to the home?

Evie: That will be lovely. Look after yourself. Bye dear.

I visit Evie almost weekly for the next four years. She has a pretty face and a very gentle voice. Her recall of her life is so precise, she recounts with minute details events in her life and describes clearly the people she encountered throughout her life.

Mina: Evie, hello, can I come in?

Evie: Hello dear, yes do ... come in ... there's a chair ... over there.

Mina: How have you been ... Evie? ...

Evie: Oh dear ... not so good today ...

Mina: What do you mean ... not so good ... any pain?

Evie: No ... not pain ... I guess ... pain in the head ... (Evie chuckles, but not quite so cheerfully as in my last visit).

Mina: Do you want to tell me about it?

Evie: What's your name dear?

Mina:	Mina, Evie ... my name is Mina.
Evie:	Nina ... of course ... that's a nice name ...
Mina:	(I sit by Evie's bedside and we hold hands) Can I get you anything Evie ... cup of tea ... glass of water ....?
Evie:	I'd really like one of those chocolates ... over there ... can you see them? I can't see them myself ... (Evie had very poor eyesight).
Mina:	There you are ... now ... would you like to tell me what's upsetting you, Evie? ... or is it too private to tell me?
Evie:	Oh no dear, nothing private ... I just am tired ... tired of being here ...
Mina:	Do you mean ... tired of living Evie?
Evie:	Yes ... that's it ... that's it exactly ...
Mina:	Do you want to die, Evie?
Evie:	(Evie nods and looks at me with damp eyes) oh yes ... why am I still here?
Mina:	I don't know Evie ... I don't know ... why do you want to die, Evie ...?
Evie:	I can't move ... I can't see ... I don't understand why him up there hasn't called me yet ... (Evie chuckles a little more cheerfully this time).
Mina:	You mean God?
Evie:	Oh yes ... him up there (Evie points to the ceiling).
Mina:	You believe in God then, Evie?
Evie:	Oh yes, very much so ... do you?
Mina:	Yes, I do, Evie ... but I am not very religious ... I go to church a few times a year ... what about you?... did you go to church before you came here?
Evie:	Oh yes ... I loved it ... but I always felt guilty about going?

Mina: Why, Evie? Why did you feel guilty?

Evie: Well, I don't think I should have gone ... not really ... I wasn't a proper Christian ... not really ...

Mina: I don't understand, Evie ... are you Church of England or Roman Catholic, or some other branch of Christianity?

Evie: Oh, Church of England...

Mina: So, what makes you think that you shouldn't have been going to church ... that you were not a proper Christian...

Evie: Well. I'm a bit ashamed, but I was never confirmed a Christian?

Mina: Does that matter? You were baptised, were you?

Evie: Well, I think so; my mother told me I was baptised ... she used to take me to church every Sunday.

Mina: Well then ...

Evie: Well then ... I'll tell you a story ... a secret story ...

Mina: About your confirmation?

Evie: (Evie nods) well ... I'd gone to all the Sunday school sessions to prepare for the confirmation ... had learnt all the lessons ... . On the Sunday morning of the confirmation ... I ran, because I was late ... I opened the heavy door a bit ... because I was late ... and there they were ... all the girls ... same as me ... all dressed in white ... and I couldn't go in ... . Nobody saw me ... so I closed the door and went ....

Mina: You didn't go in?

Evie: No.

Mina: Why Evie, why didn't you go in?

Evie: Well, I didn't have a white dress ... I thought maybe some other girls might not have a white dress ... but there they were ... all in white ....

Mina: What happened after that?

Evie: Well, the vicar asked me ... next time he saw me ... that he hadn't seen me at the confirmation ... (Evie chuckles here a bit cheekily) I didn't think he'd notice that I wasn't there ... so he wanted to know why I hadn't turned up ...

Mina: And what did you say?

Evie: I told him the truth ....

Mina: And what did he say?

Evie: He said that I should have gone in ... that God would not have minded ... and that ... if I had told him before ... they would have found a white dress for me anyway ...

Mina: And you didn't try again to be confirmed?

Evie: No, I never was ...

Mina: Does that upset you?

Evie: Oh yes, I would have like it ...

Mina: Would you like us to look into it now ... if you could be confirmed?

Evie: Do you think it would be possible?

Mina: One can only try, Evie. I'll talk to the managers and see what they say ... shall I?

Evie: Okay dear ... that would be nice ...

Mina: Perfect ... I'll leave you to rest now, Evie ... I'll see you next time?

Evie: (Evie smiles her goodbye).

I discuss Evie's wishes with the administrator who quickly ascertains from a local church that enquiries will be made with the diocese bishop.

MINA DREVER

Mina:	Good morning, Evie, you look good today ....
Evie:	Hello dear, how lovely to see you. What's it like outside?
Mina:	It's very bright and sunny, Evie ...
Evie:	I thought it was ... I can feel the brightness in the air ... is the window open?
Mina:	Yes, it is ... would you like me to shut it, Evie?
Evie:	No, it's okay ...
Mina:	Tell me how you've been, Evie, this last week.
Evie:	I've been fine ... my daughter came on Sunday; we had lunch together here ...
Mina:	Wonderful ... where does your daughter live?
Evie:	In Bishop's Stortford.
Mina:	Not far ... is that where you lived, Evie, before you came here?
Evie:	No, we lived in Takely, in a mobile home ...
Mina:	Sounds romantic ...
Evie:	Oh, it was; we loved out mobile home ...
Mina:	And where did you live before coming to Takely, Evie?
Evie:	Oh, all over the place ...
Mina:	Where did you live with your parents? ...
Evie:	My mother died when I was three ... so we moved around a bit ...
Mina:	That must have been very sad for you ...
Evie:	It was ...
Mina:	Did your father marry again?
Evie:	Eventually ... but I went to live with my aunt ... we went to Nottinghamshire ...
Mina:	Was she good to you ... your aunt?
Evie:	Oh yes ... she did her best (Evie chuckles with an impish smile!).

72

Mina:	Were you a bit of a handful? ...
Evie:	A bit ... (Evie smiles and lifts her shoulders) ... what about you dear ... tell me about you ...
Mina:	Oh, I am good, thank you, Evie; I went to church on Sunday, for the first time in ages.
Evie:	That's nice ... did you say a prayer for me ...
Mina:	Of course, Evie ... a catholic prayer Evie... does it count?
Evie:	I suppose (we laugh together) ... what do you think?
Mina:	About what?
Evie:	What's your name again?
Mina:	Mina, m for mother, I, n for no, a ... Mina.
Evie:	Nina ... that's a nice name ... ... what do you think Nina?
Mina:	About what?
Evie:	About why he (Evie points up to the ceiling) ... why he doesn't call me yet.
Mina:	Ah, I don't know ... maybe it's not your time yet ... maybe you haven't finished your job yet on this earth.
Evie:	My job? .... I have done nothing for years ... I am just lying here ... I'm no good to anyone ...
Mina:	Well, maybe he thinks otherwise ...
Evie:	I don't know ... I'm just a speck of dust ... yes ... a speck of dust ...
Mina:	That's a beautiful image ... but you don't mean use-less surely?
Evie:	Oh yes, useless speck of dust ...
Mina:	Ah, but maybe you ... that's exactly your job ... to enable all these young people here to learn from you how to be kind, and how to care for people in a

	gentle way ... how to listen and how to talk to people who, like you, are completely dependent on others for a tender word and a warm hug ...
Evie:	Do you think so?
Mina:	Yes, I do ... some people ... I have read somewhere ... there are those ... from all sorts of religions ... who believe that we each have a job to do on earth ... and we die only when we have completed it ...
Evie:	Do you believe it?
Mina:	Yeah ... I think I do ... my job today is to make you smile ...
Evie:	Well, you did that dear ... you made me smile ...
Mina:	And now you are tired ... I can see that ... so I'll see you next time?
Evie:	That will be nice ... you take care ....
Mina:	I will, Evie ... I will ... bye

The last time I see Evie, is on the morning of her death. I arrive at the care home, and I am immediately told that Evie has reached her end of life. I go into her room. I sit by her bedside and take her hand. I stay with Evie until her daughter arrives.

Mina:	Hello Evie, it's Mina ...
	Evie turns her head towards me, opens her eyes, smiles a beautiful smile and points her index finger straight up towards the sky ... she is telling me that He has finally come to take her away from this land. She looks radiant.

Evie's real name was Yvonne. I always knew her as Evie. This is what her daughter Susan said in her reply to my request for permission to publish these conversations with her mum:

> 'I am very happy to give permission for this inclusion to go ahead … Mum loved to be called Evie, so that's lovely Mina'

In memory of Evie and her fervent faith, the care home manager, Sue King, created an altar along one corridor. On the wall was a large, framed jigsaw puzzle of an angel that Evie had constructed at some point in her life and that had hung in her room all the years she lived at Redbond Lodge. Candles and religious reading were placed on the altar and there was a kneeling stool for those who wished to stop and read and remember.

LAST WORD

It is not possible to do justice to the many people with whom I was privileged to share their remembered lives. All these conversations are but very small representations of the countless voices who told me their most inner thoughts, wishes and desires, as well as their greatest fears. I enjoyed the confidences of many a Jean, Ronald, John, Peter, Henry, Mary, Susan ... to mention just a few names.

All of them had many things in common: fear of the unknown, bittersweet acceptance of their reality, sadness at the loss of their former selves, frustration at not being heard and understood, resentment at being so dependent on the generosity of spirit of others.

Many of them feel abandoned by their families. Many of them expressed these feelings very clearly. Even those who understood that their children and husbands or wives or grandchildren have to live their own lives experience a strong sense of being left behind.

The most magnanimous and stoical of us cannot comprehend what that must feel like ... until it happens to us.

My wish is for readers of these conversations to stop for a second, before they express impatience or intolerance in tone if not in words, to imagine what it must feel like to be completely reliant on others' goodwill.

ACKNOWLEDGEMENTS

My warmest thanks to all the people who allowed me to sit with them and share their mental life with me and to their families who gave me permission to publish.

I would like to thank above all others Sue King, until August 2021 the manager at Redbond Lodge Residential Care Home in Great Dunmow, for her unquestioning belief in my ideas and for supporting them unflinchingly. None of this would have been re-alised without Sue's passionate commitment. Thank you, Sue.

Of the word *Amelesia,* Sue says:

> I really love the wording chosen instead of using demen-tia. Amelesia is a much kinder word. It would be lovely to use it worldwide and stop the stigma associated with dementia.

You can read more about Amelesia on my website www.ame-lesia.com

You can email me on minadrever@aol.com

AUTHOR PROFILE

Mina lives in Essex in England. Her professional life was in education before she started her work on Dementia. Most of her time is spent between reading and writing about Dementia and visiting residents in Redbond Residential Care Home in Great Dunmow. Mina's aim is to turn upside down our idea of Dementia. She believes that only by dropping this negative word will we begin to see that people with impaired cognitive skills are not mad. They are simply prone to unmindfulness, to be 'absent' from our 'now'.

For more information on this work, please visit Mina's website: www.amelesia.com

You are invited to contribute your thoughts on Dementia on the Forum page of the Amelesia website

You can also write to Mina on: minadrever@aol.com

Printed in Great Britain
by Amazon